THE MIGHTY LITTLE BOOK

MYKELL
WILSON

Editor: Karen Rowe, KarenRowe.com
Cover Design: Shake Creative, ShakeTampa.com
Inside Layout: Ljiljana Pavkov

Printed in the United States
ISBN: 978-1-5323-0969-4

CONTENTS

DEDICATION

THE BOOK IS DEDICATED TO THE READER.

May you find a gentle light to ignite your flame and fuel to keep your fire going.

ACKNOWLEDGMENTS

IT SOUNDS CLICHÉ BUT I WANT TO GIVE HONOR TO GOD. It is the lasting opportunity of love that fuels dreams and builds people. The power of His love has caused me to come alive and embellished my life with favor. My connection to God and my awareness of His purpose for my life motivates me to become the man necessary to live out this purpose.

MUCH LOVE TO MY SPIRITUAL MENTORS:
Touré Roberts, Phil Munsey and Bob Hazlett.

TO ALL OF THOSE WITH WHOM I WORK IN
ministry and leadership, thank you.

TO MY FRIENDS AND FAMILY AND ALL OF THE
mighty people who support me, knowingly or
unknowingly, I honor you.

THANK YOU ALL WHO PURCHASE AND READ THIS
book, your investment in my dream and legacy are
vital to me.

A NOTE TO READERS

HAVE YOU EVER WANDERED DOWN A STREET, NOT really knowing where you're going, only to discover the most amazing bar, bookstore, restaurant or boutique? The creation of this book has been kind of like that.

I ALWAYS HAVE BEEN A SOCIAL PERSON, SO SOCIAL media was a natural fit for me. While I find that many of the posts are inspiring, the true question is WHAT is being inspired? Most things seen online move people to wish they were something they are not — fitter, thinner, married, more famous — or wish they had something they don't — more wealth, a better car, different colored eyes or a dog they don't have time for. These things are great, of course, but it's our ability to discern between healthy motivation and "unhealthy" desires (that point to areas that are broken or lack a healthy drive to improve or succeed) that shape our inner growth.

I LOVE PEOPLE AND I BELIEVE WE ALL HAVE MIGHT in us that simply needs a moment of activation. That moment is the flame that ignites a mighty fire in our lives. For me, understanding the void of healthy motivation motivated me to inspire others. I started writing daily posts about life, self-development, overcoming adversity and positivity on Twitter, Instagram and Facebook. The impact they were having on people all over the world led me to gather some of my favorite and most circulated posts. I now present to you in book form my best compilation of inspirational-momentum; transforming fuel for your fire.

LIVE INSPIRED,

MYKELL

PART 1

LIVE

LOVE

Love intentionally.

No one should have
to earn what was also
a gift to us.

A TRUE DESIRE TO IMPACT THE WORLD IS TO FIND the humility to love everyone in it. If you limit your love, it isn't love at all.

Your ability to be patient reveals your willingness to love.

LOVE ALWAYS TAKES THAT EXTRA SECOND, ONE more step. When we remember none of us are perfect it's easier to make the CHOICE to love where we would normally resort to anger/frustration. When we know we can change the atmosphere, we won't get so caught up in changing people. Making the focus love isn't being passive, it's being wise, because ultimately the people we are dealing with have as much value as ourselves.

WE ALL WANT TO BE FAMOUS.

WE ARE ORDINARY PEOPLE LIVING EXTRAORDINARILY in God's love. When we place more than a person was designed to carry, we steal their right to be loved just like we are loved, their chance to discover what's "right" and become it, not just do it. They miss out on the opportunity that's sometimes only found in making mistakes. When we judge more than we love or complain more than we pray, we miss our opportunity to live like Jesus lived and to love how He loves. Do you want to be the doctor or the scalpel? Don't cut what your love won't heal.

FRIENDSHIP

RELATIONSHIPS ARE BUILT ON THE SACRIFICE OF investment, the pavement of love. No one is perfect and none of us ever will be, but the seed of love can birth a forest of life. Friends must make a choice to love each other, challenge each other and to NEVER GIVE UP on one another. You can't walk out because any of you have issues, you carry the love and you'll carry each other to growth. If your friends don't keep it real and inspire solutions not just point out problems, you probably need new friends. If you don't better yourself for the sake of them, you probably aren't a good friend. Friends aren't fans, they are those who love the true you and settle for nothing less than the person you have the potential to be.

A HEART POURED OUT IS A HEART FULL.

DON'T WAIT TO LOVE. IT'S A PRIVILEGE NOT A right. We have no love because we only give it away as people earn it. We tally the good we give and expect people to pay us back. We withhold it because we're mad and we even hide it because we want to look tough. We're the ones missing out because we can't gain what we never learned to carry.

Love finds the wind through the storm and sails far above the deepest dangers.

DIDN'T MEAN TO END UP HERE, BUT I WILL LOVE FROM HERE.

WE CROSS PATHS SO OFTEN WITH THE SAME PEOPLE and have the CHOICE to either see a face or experience the beauty of exchange. Don't limit your life to the faces around you, invest in the heart of them and you'll discover life was more than a period of survival, it was an infinite moment of Love.

IF WE LOOK FOR MORE REASONS TO LOVE PEOPLE WE WILL FIND LESS REASONS TO HATE THEM.

EVERYONE'S A CRITIC AND THERE ARE TOO MANY fans. We need more lovers, honest, supporting and guiding. Love doesn't harshly judge or simply agree with everything, it becomes the answer and asks questions that build better people.

Don't wait until people are perfect TO LOVE THEM. Your love could be the vehicle that carries people TO LOVE'S PERFECT HEALING.

DON'T WAIT. LOVE, ACTUALLY. THEY MAY NEVER get it right or apologize. You may never feel qualified. Nevertheless, Everyone is worth being loved. If you have the humility to FIND WORTH in people and invest, their value will have no debt. Love heals what judgment, disappointment and offense can't even mend.

Every person you come across is another opportunity to Love. Let your life declare love exists.

REAL LOVE LOOKS FOR THE OPPORTUNITY TO BE what it is. It doesn't wait to apologize and doesn't need to be right to have the humility to manage someone else's heart! It finds dark places and lights them up and repairs what is broken. It's not an opportunist and doesn't find glory in itself, it finds glory in all those it touches and leads them to the best parts of themselves. Try loving for real today. Love All, not just those you feel you're supposed to.

WHAT THEY SAY ABOUT YOU WHEN YOU'RE GONE REVEALS WHO YOU WERE WHEN YOU WERE THERE.

BE KNOWN FOR YOUR HEART. CHARACTER WILL always trump any award because it's not the destinations we arrive to that God wants to use but the people He leads there. Be mighty in Love.

YOU WILL KNOW HOW MUCH SOMEONE LOVES YOU BY THEIR SACRIFICE, NOT WHAT'S CONVENIENT. A TRUE OFFERING IS OFTEN FOUND IN SACRIFICE.

WHAT YOU'RE WILLING TO SPEND DETERMINES the value of your love. If your love costs...

LOVE: IT'S A CHOICE, NOT A FEELING!

IF YOU CAN TURN IT OFF, YOU'VE SETTLED FOR never becoming what you could have. If you only give it when you feel like it, you lack the ability to give it to those who don't feel at all.

DON'T ALLOW YOUR OPINION TO GOVERN YOUR ABILITY TO LOVE. DON'T LET YOUR LOVE STOP AT YOU.

THE WAY TO LOVE IS THROUGH THE SURRENDER OF self. When we can give even ourselves, we will give the best we have to offer. That's Love.

BE KNOWN FOR YOUR HEART.

WHEN I WEIGH LIFE AND THE GLORY OF IT, I'VE discovered the greatest achievement is gaining the heart of God and living from that place, with Him receiving the glory. In a world where we can be anything and have it all, why not strive to do it all.... with Love?

Love is always looking
for an opportunity to be,
it doesn't need a holiday
and pride is its enemy.
Love doesn't take
account of its actions,
it wants for you more
than it wants you. Even
when it's right, it meets
you where you're wrong.
Love heals.
It's the true Medicine
of life. Love won't relent.
Love is.

DON'T TURN YOUR LOVE OFF. AT ANY COST DIE to love and you'll live to love again. I've learned love is to be cherished and I've learned I'm irreplaceable.

LOVE
DOESN'T
RETALIATE.

IT
COMMUNICATES.

If you live to love,
you'll love your life.
For the greatest
rewards in life
come from the
WILLINGNESS
TO GIVE.

HEAVY LOVE. DON'T TURN YOUR LOVE OFF.

WE FEAR LOVING
BECAUSE WE
FEAR BEING
HURT BUT MORE
THAN PAIN WE
SHOULD FEAR
THE FAILURE
TO LOVE.

DISCOVER HOW TO LOVE AND LEARN HOW TO LOVE unconditionally. The gift of love is the maturity and willingness to sacrifice yourself and your offense, opinion, desires and wants for the opportunity to love. Love doesn't take account of what it's doing, it just is.

If Hitler can send the world to war then one man, possibly you or I, can send the world to Love.

WHAT HAVE YOU DONE FOR YOUR HOME, community and city? The PEOPLE?! What will you do? Everyone has a special mantle to bless the world, and it's different for each individual. If we hold ourselves accountable BEyond our success, we will find an opportunity to revolutionize Love. If we build better people we will have a better world. It doesn't start with the bad guys, it starts with us! We are the answer to the problems we see!

33

People change and with time things become beautiful. Love never gives up; people do. Don't quit.

THE WAR IS NOT WITH LOVE. THE WAR IS WITHIN ourselves. When we mature, we find that love is worth the sacrifice of pride, the boldness of humility and the surrender of emotions, for what we can give qualifies us for what we can receive. Love is worth it all because It is the only absolute truth.

IF YOU CAN'T EVEN MANAGE THE HEARTS OF THOSE WHO LOVE YOU WHAT CRUELTY WILL YOU DO TO THOSE THAT DON'T?

CHECK YOUR HEART. BE ACCOUNTABLE TO LOVE.

LOVE IS A RISK ALWAYS
WORTH TAKING, FOR
TO HAVE LOVED AND
FELT A TRUTH SO DEEP
OUTWEIGHS THE PRIDE
TO SURRENDER.

NEVER STOP LOVING.

A CLOUD OF LOVE CAN WASH AWAY ANY HURT.
True healing begins with the gift and opportunity
to Love.

I believe
in MIRACLES
because
I believe
in LoVE.

LOVE PEOPLE ENOUGH
TO GIVE THEM SPACE
TO GROW WITHOUT
THE RIGHTEOUSNESS
OF YOUR OPINION.

SOME THINGS
AREN'T ABOUT
WHO'S RIGHT
OR WRONG.

LOVE IS HAVING
PATIENCE
ENOUGH TO
COMMUNICATE
EVEN WHEN
YOU FEEL
YOU SHOULDN'T
HAVE TO.

TO RECEIVE LOVE
IS GREAT AND TO
KNOW YOU'RE LOVED
IS CONFIRMING
BUT TO GIVE LOVE,
NOW THAT'S A LIFE
WELL SPENT.

FAITH

The greatest thing we can do is **LEAD** another to have a conversation with **GOD.**

Discovering
the need for God
is finding your
STRENGTH.

PERFECTION DOESN'T EXIST BECAUSE THERE IS NO limit to the people we can become. For this reason, we don't wallow in our deficiencies and we don't glory in our good deeds. We live life willing to become and at peace with the process it takes.

Don't fear
what you
cannot see.

Seeds grow
in unseen
places.

It's not enough to just believe in God, at some point you have to START LIVING FOR HIM.

FAITH IS THE BEGINNING OF A JOURNEY OF transformation; we must check ourselves to ensure we are increasing our understanding of what we believe. Love is the foundation of any relationship but it doesn't end there. From that foundation, something tangible is built. Don't stop your faith at the blueprint of your willingness. Find the courage to BUILD and dwell in the tabernacle of relationship.

ESTABLISH THE VOICE

PRAYER IS THE VOICE OF RELATIONSHIP. YOU TALK at those who don't know you, and you only listen to those you're trying to understand. Those you carry relationship with form an abiding exchange that never runs dry and is always willing to find total alignment. Investing in prayer is to invest in relationship and the way to find your voice.

HAVE MORE FAITH IN WHAT YOU CANNOT SEE because what you can see, at best, is the glory of an old idea.

HAVE YOU SETTLED FOR "GOD'S WILL?"

PEOPLE OF FAITH OFTEN BELIEVE "GOD CAN DO IT" but the problem is they stop at what He can do and never take OWNERSHIP for what they want and can do with God. The fear to believe and the pride of false humility says, "whatever God wants I want," but to truly say that is to also say "I know who I am and what I want." God is about relationship and development not slavery and hindrance. We don't have to fear what we want or ask from God because God is in our desires when we have the willingness to bring the HONESTY of what we want before Him. "Seeking ye first the kingdom" (Matthew 6:33) isn't about disregarding what we want but placing it at His feet and trusting He can and will do it. He grants what we ask and is excited to please because He gets to steer the process, and the process builds relationship. Where failing to move doesn't grant the opportunity, God doing it alone removes our gifted ability and doing it outside of God leaves us to govern what's larger than us. Ask and you'll receive, create and you'll have.

PRAYER

PRAYER IS FAR FROM A LIST OF "I NEED" AND "I wish," it's a time where we can set aside EVERYTHING to have conversation and exchange. You don't have to be perfect to pray and you don't have to be great with words, you just need to be willing to open your heart to how you really feel. Such transparency gives freedom to receive (instructions to live and win) and the opportunity to release whatever you may need (fear, doubt, joy, secrets that are killing you). Spend more time talking to God and I promise you will discover a kingdom language that will allow you to speak to the obstacles and fears of life! Prayer is the communication of love and worship is the space to speak.

Live in Expectation. Amazing things happen when God's timing meets our faith.

IF WE HAVE FAITH BUT LACK THE ALIGNMENT OF God we will grow weary in well-doing. If God releases provision to us and our faith is immature, our blessing will overtake our capacity. Success is found when our faith has matured IN THE WAY of God's divine timing. We need both. Seek wisdom and keep dreaming. God is always one step higher than our faith and that's why faith always requires the sacrifice of GROWTH. If you're being tested/stretched, KEEP HOPE and you will arrive to the next level of your becoming within God's willingness. God didn't create us to suffer, He granted us the opportunity to overcome our sufferings and to not live as robots and slaves but in relationship and royalty.

'With all of the beautiful things we can accomplish, if we do so without God none of them even matter.

MATTHEW 6:33: THE GOAL ISN'T TO "HAVE THINGS added," but to be so full you need nothing but the opportunity to give. Seeking God first keeps you whole and unneedy.

WHEN GOD IS MAXIMIZED IN US NOTHING ELSE CAN FIT.

THE ANSWER TO CHANGE (INSIDE AND OUT, NOT just external "success") is found in our relationship with God. When we spend time with Him, our identity is realized. In that place, everything outside of who we are must detach itself. When I feel weak, or that life is lacking, I don't beat myself up, I use that fight to climb a little higher where God is. The goal isn't to be perfect but to rest in His perfect love. Light drowns darkness.

AT THE END OF OUR ABILITY WE FIND GOD'S CAPABILITY.

WHEN WE GIVE OUT OF OUR SCARCITY, OUR FAITH offers up WHAT WE CURRENTLY HAVE and places it in the heavenly realm where we have supernatural access to limitless resources for our needs. Win today by offering it up in faith for tomorrow.

If you remain focused on what God is doing you'll be less distracted with what/how long it's taking.

MOST OF THE EXTERNAL SUCCESS WE SEE TOOK AN internal sacrifice. When we place our focus on that which is becoming, that which has been is easy to let go of. If you find you're in a season of SACRIFICE AND OBSTACLE it's because the old you can't fit into the NEW space God has for you. Like a key, there is a perfect shape of YOU that WILL UNLOCK THE DOOR. Be transformed.

GOD IS THE SOURCE. EVERYTHING ELSE IS A RESOURCE.

ALL OUR BLESSINGS COME FROM GOD. THE industry is always telling us who to be and what's expected, it's important to KNOW and NEVER LOSE SIGHT of who we are. The only place to be is right where God desires us to be. Sometimes we must even abandon our own plans to live in the place of purpose; the only true destination of life.

WIN YOUR MIND AND YOU WILL WIN THE WAR. OFTEN THE TRUE BATTLE ISN'T WHAT YOU'RE FACING BUT WHAT YOU'RE THINKING.

WORSHIP, PRAISE AND THANKSGIVING ARE THE keys to freedom.

1. WORSHIP: STAY FOCUSED ON GOD AND everything else becomes small.

2. PRAISE: CELEBRATE THROUGH IT ALL AND BUILD new strength over and over.

3. THANKSGIVING: REMAIN THANKFUL FOR IT ALL. The humility found in small things adds up to the glory of large things.

Sometimes God conceals the big picture to protect it. Don't sabotage your entire life because you didn't have even enough faith for today.

CAN YOUR FAITH BIRTH YOUR DREAM? GOD HAD planned to make Abraham's seed a mighty nation. At the time, Abraham and his wife Sarah had no children. When God told Sarah, in her old age, she would bear a child, she didn't believe Him. If she had not had faith enough to believe God for a small miracle (a son), she definitely would not have had faith to believe God for the fullness He was going to do (create a mighty nation).

GOD WON'T GIVE YOU WHAT WILL DISTRACT YOU FROM HIM BUT HE WILL ALWAYS GIVE YOU WHAT WILL LEAD YOU TO HIM. GOD WILL ONLY GIVE YOU WHAT YOU ARE WILLING TO GIVE AWAY, FOR WHAT YOU TREASURE DETERMINES WHAT WILL GOVERN YOUR HEART.

THE OBJECT OF YOUR FAITH BECOMES THE GOD of your life.

YES GOD.

SAY IT AND MEAN IT. IT'S TIME FOR A LIFE CHANGE. You need it. You're tired and you don't have to be anymore. Receive the Love today.

IF YOU KEEP PUTTING PEOPLE IN YOUR LIFE YOU won't have room for the people God needs in your life, people who are pure and purpose-led.

SOMETIMES YOU NEED TO FALL TO FIND GOD WAS carrying you, not your own strength. True testimony is surrender not perfection.

WHEN YOU SEE AN IMPOSSIBLE SITUATION, LOOK again, you'll see a God opportunity. Your impossible is God's opportunity.

LORD, WHERE DO YOU WANT ME TO GO?! Sometimes the prayer isn't "what do you want me to do?" it's "where do you want me to go?" That will reveal what must be done.

FALL IN FAITH AND TRUST GOD ENOUGH TO FAIL. THE TRUE REWARD OF FAITH IS FAITH!

WHEN WE FEAR STARVING IN THE NEST MORE THAN we fear the fall we will discover our ability to fly. The ability to fly is found in a baby bird's instinct but only activated in its fall. By design, instinct exists but it is by faith potential takes flight. Don't fear falling, it's the first step to you flying!!!

PART II
LOVE
YOURSELF

IDENTITY

WHAT YOU ALLOW TO VALIDATE YOU BECOMES THE INDICATOR OF YOUR SUCCESS. THEREFORE, WHEN YOU KNOW YOU WERE BORN A WINNER, IT'S NOT A QUESTION IF YOU'LL FINISH THE RACE, IT'S JUST A MATTER OF WIN (WHEN)!

HAVE A WINNING MINDSET. YOUR MIND MAKES the difference!

MY PAIN HAS PRODUCED MUCH PROGRESS because in finding the courage to go on I found who I am, a winner.

You'll NeVeR lose wHeN you believe you weRe BORN A WINNER.

WE SPEND MOST OF OUR TIME QUESTIONING IF something is possible but we can only receive according to who we perceive ourselves to be. Our mindset dictates the perception of what we have. No matter what, if I gave you a million dollars and you believed it was ten dollars, you would never attempt to spend its worth. If you go into every situation with a mindset of doubt or failure you've labeled who you are as such. When your mindset is that you've already won you will run the race with joy instead of desperation; there is no arrival when you realize YOU are already here. Now just be!

DESTINY WILL ALWAYS SPEAK TO THE DEPTHS OF WHO YOU ARE AND WHEN YOU HAVE THE COURAGE TO LISTEN, YOU CAN SCREAM TO THE WORLD WHO YOU WERE BORN TO BE. HONOR YOUR CREATION.

YOU'RE LOCKED IN LOVE.

THE KEY TO LIFE IS KNOWING WHO YOU ARE, knowing the One who made you and discovering the Love that keeps you in relationship. Forever locked in love.

WHO DID YOU INTENTIONALLY MAKE SMILE TODAY? LOVE INTENTIONALLY.

IF YOU WAIT FOR SOMEONE TO DESERVE YOUR love before you make the choice to give your love, you lack the understanding of love. It's a gift to be given, not hoarded. It's more of a privilege TO LOVE than it is for someone to receive your love.

WHAT MAKES WOMEN POWERFUL ISN'T THE PROOF that they can "do what men do," but the embracing of what makes them different from men and adding that to sexuality and the world. One's strength is always found in their uniqueness, not their ability to duplicate what already is. I love women for who they are, who they can be and I uplift who they will be! Invest in the women around you. Check my video too!!

out of all the grains
of sand, not one
is the sun.

DISCOVER YOU.

STOP LOOKING, STOP COUNTING, STOP comparing, stop settling, stop complaining, stop resting on your talent and start being. You are unique and you add value. No one else is like you, which means the world NEEDS YOU! But how could you ever give away what you haven't first received? Discover YOU and journey it through history.

IDENTITY IS THE KEY TO FREEDOM.

THE DESTINY OF GREAT MEN IS FOUND ALONG THE roads never traveled, for no one will ever truly understand another's personal sacrifice. Such sacrifice, that we all have available to us, is to be embraced, although it can cause us to feel isolated. I've learned the isolation isn't about screaming, "we are alone," but about shaping us unadulterated from the world. The "world" isn't bad and we are each here to ADD TO IT not simply become what already is. In our identity, our true selves are all we need to succeed and overcome everything. Often trials are more about doing the right things than they are about beating ourselves up over doing the wrong things. A slight shift in perspective will FREE YOU and cause YOU to FIND a smooth path to inner growth that always leads to outer achievement. Today, AGAIN, say YES TO YOU!

When you aren't afraid of risk, change or rejection, you find there's life after death and the sky at the end of the road.

IF YOU FIND YOU'RE FEARFUL TO MAKE NECESSARY changes in your life, understand that courage is only needed where life appears impossible. Overcoming obstacles is more about understanding who you are than simply knowing what you stand in need of. Find who you really are (the inside) and you'll find the strength to get what you really want (the outside). Look within to win.

THINK LEGACY: YOU'LL FIND IT EASIER TO FACE YOUR OBSTACLES, YOU'LL BE MORE EXCITED TO BE A TESTIMONY OF VICTORY THAN YOU ARE TIRED OF FIGHTING THE BATTLE.

DON'T SETTLE FOR THE LOWER YOU BECAUSE IT'S comfortable, live for the higher you. Your life can be an open door of freedom for the generations to come. The legacy of tomorrow is worth your sacrifice now.

WHEN YOU KNOW WHO YOU ARE YOU TRULY UNDERSTAND WHO YOU ARE NOT!

IDENTITY IS FREEDOM. THE WORLD IS ALWAYS telling us who to be; skeptics and spectators are everywhere. We've allowed the bad AND good times of life to disqualify/qualify our joy. We have believed when others or even ourselves have said we are ugly, broke, sinners, unloved, stupid and more! TODAY, WIN. Look in the mirror and speak to the REAL YOU. You've lived beneath yourself long enough. TODAY, declare you are mighty, powerful and whatever else you need to embrace to live happy, overflowing, complete and progressing. Believe you are meant for a great life inside and out NOW!

Don't use "this is who I am" as an excuse to live carelessly. Who you are should see who you're not!

LOVING YOURSELF ISN'T LIVING IN THE ACCEPTANCE of your flaws, but embracing the challenge to progress through them.

It's OK to have fear, it's NOT OK to embrace the identity of it. Light is light even in darkness.

DON'T BECOME WHAT YOU SEE, INSTEAD CAUSE what you're looking at to transform into what YOU WANT it to be. Don't let life just happen to you... Happen to life! Your identity is your victory.

WHO ARE YOU REALLY?

WHERE YOU PLACE YOUR TIME IS WHERE YOU SERVE and where you serve reveals who you are.

SEE WHAT THEY CAN'T

EVEN IF THE WORLD NEVER LOOKS AT YOU, KNOW you exist. Growth begins where your ego dies and true confidence is found where peace in you resides.

Pose for the camera!!

WE ALL WANT TO WALK THE RED CARPET AND BE seen but it's the empty hallways of our lives that give us space to know who we are when no one is watching. We are blessed because every day is another day to strive for maximized potential. Let opportunity be an extension of who you are, not the definition.

DON'T ALLOW WHAT YOU SAW TO BLUR WHAT YOU CAN SEE. WHAT YOU FOCUS ON BECOMES THE REALITY YOU'LL RECEIVE.

OUR IDENTITY REVEALS OUR VICTORY. THE reflection we see reveals who we are. If we only look at our problems how will we ever KNOW who we are? The goal isn't for problems to disappear but for you to show up. BE bigger.

SELF-LOVE

THEY MAY NOT ACTUALLY LOVE YOU, THAT'S OK! YOU LOVE YOU.

STOP INVESTING YOUR ENERGY IN DESIRING PEOPLE to care for you. Place that expectation more into loving yourself and you'll be so full you'll never need anyone to love you, just to love will be enough. Invest in you and give to others. Love fully!

IF THE PEOPLE AROUND YOU
(FLOATERS) ARE FINE WITH
YOU LIVING IN MEDIOCRITY
AND NEVER CHALLENGE
YOUR POTENTIAL, YOU NEED
NEW FRIENDS/COMPANY.
BE SURROUNDED AND
SUPPORTED BY THOSE WHO
DON'T SETTLE FOR WHO YOU
ARE NOW BUT ARE INVESTED
IN THE YOU YOU'RE GOING
TO BE; THE YOU YOU'RE
SUPPOSED TO BE.

GIVE EVERYONE THE LOVE IN YOUR HEART BUT BE
very careful with who you let hold your heart. The
same applies to life. Not everyone is fit to pour
into your life and those who aren't adding are
by default taking! Love always but BE WISE and
stop wasting time spending your life on bankrupt
investments.

INSERT selfie
Photo Here

WITH ME. EMBRACE BEING ALONE BECAUSE IN
isolation you have space to grow. Learn this daily
-- alone doesn't have to mean you're lonely, you're
just separated for the beauty of growing. Living a
little higher today, eagles fly alone.

New day?
* iNseRt aNotheR
selfie heRe *

RATHER BE FELT THAN SEEN. THE PURPOSE ISN'T
always found on the platform but in the trenches
holding it up. There's a time for everything so
embrace every season and live your year(s) fully.

Exercise:
look in the mirror,
speak POSITIVE
affirmations and
CHALLENGE
yourself!

WHEN YOU CAN FACE YOURSELF, ALL OF YOUR fears, your true, unadjusted dreams, all of your weaknesses, all of your strengths, everything bad and everything good... there you will find a champion staring back at you. Keep living!

I'M IRREPLACEABLE.

ONE OF THE GREATEST TRUTHS. IDENTITY IS freedom. It's never intimidated by someone else's amazing-ness and it's never insecure in its own ability to exist. I know who I am and I know that I'm loved. I know God didn't create me to be a duplicate nor to compete with others but to GROW AND LOVE. To say you're "irreplaceable" isn't to scream with pride that you're the best, but to declare in TOTAL FAITH that you matter and have a place. Every time I use my faith to dream, I'm using my life to live. I don't have to "sell out" or trade my values, I can just live. Don't waste another second living beneath yourself in any area, have a standard for yourself, not to feel qualified but to align with the awesome reality you're created in. YOU ARE IRREPLACEABLE!

*** If you wait until you're "successful" to love yourself you'll only end up loving what you do and miss out on the beauty of who you are.

DON'T PUT MORE VALUE ON WHAT YOU'RE TRYING to gain than what you already have, for the person you are today is the same person born to live tomorrow. Love yourself enough to know you are enough. Add to you but don't let what's outside define you, let who you are on the inside be the definition.

JUST BECAUSE YOU'RE TREATED LIKE LESS DOESN'T MEAN YOU HAVE TO LOVE YOURSELF ANY LESS! YOU ARE WHO YOU ARE, NOT WHAT OTHERS THINK OF YOU!

MAKING THE RIGHT CHOICE REQUIRES THE WILLINGNESS TO EXIST BEYOND THE MOMENT. SELF CONTROL IS ALSO A DESIRE.

ADDICTION
COMES IN MANY
FORMS.
STOP DOING DRUGS.
FACE YOURSELF
AND YOU'LL SEE
YOURSELF, FACE
YOUR PROBLEMS AND
YOU'LL SEE YOU'RE
BIGGER THAN THEM.

Are you running an obstacle course?

EACH LIFE COMES WITH A SET OF BATTLES designed to develop the person. Embracing your challenges is ultimately embracing the greatest you. Where you feel pain, where you feel weakness or opposition is the very same place you'll one day find strength to keep on your journey.

Don't be afraid to turn down what used to be good enough.

OUTLOOK

WHY WASTE TODAY WORRYING ABOUT TOMORROW? LIVE FREE.

WHAT'S THE POINT OF DYING BEFORE YOU EVEN live? What fills us eventually overflows and becomes what's around us. There's a difference between preparation and anticipation. One is ready to face anything while the other labels the outcome. The problem with labeling is that we then become limited ONLY to what we perceive. Live prepared but open. We can maximize today and build the strength needed for tomorrow. We don't know what tomorrow holds but today let's make the CHOICE TO LIVE.

YOU DON'T HAVE TO BE FAMOUS TO BE AMAZING.

YOU DON'T HAVE TO BE POPULAR TO BE THE BEST.

WHAT PEOPLE THINK OF YOU IS TO BE CONSIDERED, but what YOU THINK OF YOURSELF is irreplaceable. We are often looking for the right to be amazing and disqualify ourselves because our light isn't visible to our peers, but those who find our light will be that much brighter and those who don't can remain in the dark. The sun is always shining and though we wait for dawn to declare its day, its fire is never quenched and never ceases to BURN!! If you allow popularity and approval to be your gage of "amazing," when you need to grow you'll be puffed up with air and when you're full you'll forget true expansion isn't space but one's ability to overflow.

Don't let the life get the best of you, **USE** all of **LIFE** to get the best you!

IT'S THE MATURITY TO NOT ALLOW OPPOSITION to TAKE the best of you and to stay in control, through it ALL, to let every obstacle permit the opportunity to shape the better you.

GIVE UP.

WHEN YOU "GIVE UP" FROM THE PLACE OF surrender, still with an EXPECTATION OF HOPE (which is key), you expand your ability to receive what is best for you, which is sometimes greater than what you were holding on to.

SOMETIMES YOU HAVE TO LET GO TO BE ABLE TO grab and hold again. Taking a step back can give a better future perspective to run several steps forward. Giving up doesn't always mean you've failed, sometimes it's the starting point to you winning again!

WHEN YOU REMAIN POSITIVE WHAT ISN'T FOR YOU IS ONE STEP CLOSER TO WHAT'S WAITING FOR YOU.

YOUR SUCCESS IS FOUND IN YOUR PERSPECTIVE; the difference between the end of the world and a new beginning. SPEAK LIFE. EXPECT LIFE.

Stop looking outside to discover what you already have on the inside. Look within TO WIN.

I KNOW MY FAITH IS LACKING WHEN MY JOY IS predicated upon the temporary void fillers instead of what's lasting. When I find myself reaching to feel good instead of walking in the KNOWING that I am good, I stop and declare: He is able and I AM MORE THAN a conqueror. I'm speaking into my own life and not waiting for success or love from others or being noticed to begin to live. IF I'M ALIVE I'M LIVING! I am he, the one You made.

*** YOUR LOSS ISN'T YOUR FAILURE.

IF YOU FOCUS TOO MUCH ON WHAT YOU'VE LOST, you will fail to realize the space you now have to actually gain. No matter how much you lose, you can always gain and win again. Keep your head up and know that as long as you're alive, anything can happen. Let your faith and perspective lead that "anything" to a positive outcome. If you are cluttered with doubt and depression you'll leave no room to be filled with hope and joy. By default we will believe in something, why not believe for the best?

DO YOU HAVE FAITH TO SEE MILLIONS IN PENNIES

THERE ARE 100 MILLION PENNIES IN 1 MILLION Dollars. We all want the big PAYout but forget they begin with SMALL investments. Our ability to manage the small things will determine the capacity of our maturity for big things. Start today, see each small opportunity, invest in it and watch it ADD up to something worth every step.

IF YOU DIDN'T DO ANYTHING TO WAKE YOURSELF up today why doubt if the beauty of life will carry you through it?

103

PART III

RESURRECT
YOURSELF

WORD

You will receive it when you desire to USE IT more than you WANT it. Success, wealth and/or fame must not govern your heart. They are tools, not the source and should lead you to want the source.

PURE INTENTION PAVES THE WAY FOR BLESSING.
Why you desire it reveals more than acquiring it.

THE TRUE PLACE
OF REST IS IN
THE PEACE OF
MIND. TO MATURE
OUR THOUGHTS IS
TO SIMPLIFY LIFE'S
COMPLEXITIES.

BREADCRUMBS REVEAL THERE'S A TABLE NEAR, NOT THAT THERE IS A LACK OF RESOURCE.

HAVE HOPE.

TOO OFTEN, WE ARE SADDENED BY THE SMALL things we have now, even though we have BIG needs. With the right perspective, a winner's mindset, our small seeds eventually, even through the pressure of the ground, sprout up! Today let the little you have be an indication of more, not a reminder that you don't have enough.

Life is about balance:

A SPIRITUAL BASE, SOME HUMOR, THE DRAMA OF obstacles, perseverance and a little EDGE. Don't let people, status, titles or "ideas" put you in a box. Make all things pure and progressing and you'll never have to hide any part of who you are. You'll live WHOLE and free because the goal isn't to be perfect, but to never stop progressing and growing within God's perfect love for you.

Pornography — dangerous or fulfilling?

A QUICK TEACHING FROM MY PERSONAL VIEW: The root is living for Lust versus Love or rather what's temporary versus what's forever. Lust is a physical urgency while love is of a pure heart. One is focused on taking and another on giving. To be holy is to understand giving is gaining and dying is living, this is what makes God so pure. Pornography stirs lust, a temporary fix that is unsatisfying and therefore is always in need of more and leads to addiction. Anything that is so thought-consuming yet does not transform life in lasting areas such as divine purpose, character development, real fulfillment/joy, love, by default can't be healthy. It is a temporary fix and sometimes even feels really good but we must remember we aren't made for temporal things (at least our souls aren't). We are made for what's forever and deserve such. KNOW we are supposed to live from a spiritual place not a natural one. That's why we have souls in these earthen vessels (bodies). It is hard because we are still HERE having a natural experience, so the surrender it takes to have control over intense physical desires is an epic challenge, but victory is possible. It's possible because we always have the choice. We have the option to live from either a natural approach or a spiritual one. The Natural is physically tangible and easier to be seen with the naked eye but can only exist within those same realms, where living spiritually requires faith, which is harder, but can produce an infinite return. It can actually create a whole new route and/or way of living. This is why in dealing with the lusts of the mind we must renew our thinking and seek a higher realm that functions from the willingness to exist beyond the moment, live spiritually and dictate the actions of our lives. We don't have to be slaves to sex, emotions or feelings. We are pure so living as such is just accepting the choice available. I pray we ALL, self included, find the courage to not accept the norms but to reinvent them.

LIFE IS A GIFT TO
TEACH US HOW
TO LOVE GOD, HOW TO
LOVE OURSELVES
AND HOW TO LOVE
EACH OTHER.
IN THAT ORDER.

SELAH. LIVING TO LEARN.

What will people
say about YOU,
not simply what
you can do?

HAVE YOU INVESTED IN THE GROWTH OF WHO
you are or have you settled only for what you
do? How are we more self-absorbed than any
generation and yet lack substance? We should be
soaking wet and our lives, identities and hearts are
DRY! Let's make a change today.

SEX: THERE ARE MANY REASONS WHY BEING PROMISCUOUS AND EXTREMELY SEXUALLY ACTIVE CAN BE UNHEALTHY, BUT ONE THING TO TAKE NOTE OF IS THAT IF YOU WANT TO GET MARRIED AND ARE USED TO HAVING SO MANY SEXUAL PARTNERS YOU RUN THE RISK OF NEVER BEING SATISFIED; YOU WILL EXPECT THE ONE YOU LOVE TO FUNCTION LIKE THE MANY WHO WANTED TO USE YOU. RESERVING YOURSELF GIVES YOUR TRUE DESTINED HUSBAND/ WIFE THE OPPORTUNITY TO BE EXACTLY WHAT WAS CREATED FOR YOU, NOT JUST WHAT YOU NOW NEED BECAUSE YOU'VE TRIED IT ALL.

Often the people that will help you grow the most aren't the ones you'll always have the most surface fun with. Real relationships elevate your strong points AND CHALLENGE your weak ones. FUN doesn't always reveal truth, learn the difference between what you want and what you NEED.

BE AWARE IF YOU ONLY HAVE "YES" MEN AROUND you and make sure YOU STAY AUTHENTIC to NOT become one. Be bold enough to be honest, for the desire of Love should want people to actually be good not just feel good.

WHILE I'M HERE I'M GOING TO LIVE

WHAT IS LIFE AND WHAT IS ITS ENVY? MOST OF what we live isn't life at all but a draining illusion that draws us away from what it truly means to be alive. It's ok to want validation and the success of manmade currency but it's what can't be purchased or even earned that gives meaning to life. This is the meaning that motivates us to breathe life into the world around us. So when we say we're going to live, we've declared we have the capacity to see beyond what is fleeting and can pour into what is lasting. Everything costs but not everything is worth the price.

WHO YOU SPEND THE MOST TIME WITH WILL EITHER CHANGE YOU - OR YOU'LL CHANGE THEM. HEALTHY RELATIONSHIPS REQUIRE THE GROWTH OF ALL PEOPLE INVOLVED.

DO YOU NEED NEW FRIENDS? IF YOUR FRIENDS ARE up to the same non-sense they were five years ago, you need new friends. This may be difficult, but it's quintessential to your growth. It doesn't mean turn your love off, but guard your time and what you allow to influence your atmosphere. Haters, addicts, abusers, those lacking purpose, anyone lacking love and those who only praise you and never challenge you may need to be distanced from you; but never your love. Making the choice to grow isn't walking out on people, it's having enough love for self to not settle for quicksand. You can't even adequately love someone else until you love yourself. Love yourself enough to grow.

Those who sacrifice and work hard for you are worth more than those who simply praise you. Don't neglect your true fans, your friends, the ones you have in every day life, not just the ones who want to be entertained by you.

GRATITUDE THAT IS NOT SEEN MOST LIKELY WILL not be felt. If we fail to honor those fighting for us we will limit life to us, instead of the hero within us. Your life is bigger than you.

AND YET WE HANG
ON TO THE STEMS
OF ROSES KNOWING
THEY HAVE THORNS.

DON'T BELIEVE
IN WHAT YOU
WON'T LIVE FOR,
DON'T LIVE FOR
WHAT YOU
WON'T DIE FOR.

HEALING

WE HAVE A CHOICE. OUR OBSTACLES CAN BECOME OUR TOOLS OR WEAPONS USED AGAINST US.

DON'T LET YOUR PAST BECOME A HANDICAP. Scars reveal the grace of healing more than they do the damage done. We all suffer and those who use their suffering wisely blaze trails while those who wallow in them drown. You don't have to suffer. Peace is a choice, not a destination. Shift your mindset and you'll shift your life.

RESERVING A PORTION OF YOUR FAITH TO COUNTER DISAPPOINTMENT ISN'T FAITH AT ALL, IT'S DOUBT.

DO YOU REALLY BELIEVE? AT SOME POINT WE must play life offensively and not merely defensively, we must score points, not just block shots. To die is to live because in discovering the worst that can happen we find that we still have a choice to keep going. The choice is greater than the obstacle because our perception of what we're capable of becomes our fuel to succeed. Use your FAITH today - kill all doubt.

AS CRAZY AS IT
SOUNDS, BEING HURT
REVEALS THE DEPTH
OF YOUR LOVE AND
TRIALS STRENGTHEN
THE VOICE OF YOUR
PURPOSE; PREVAIL!

"LET IT BE UGLY. IT DON'T MEAN NOTHING.
Hard ain't always what it seems, cuz what
makes you beautiful Is all that you learn as
you go through."

IF DEFENSE IS YOUR
FIRST RESPONSE,
PRIDE WILL LEAD YOU
TO KILL THE VERY
PEOPLE YOU ONCE
LOVED. LET IT GO.
IF YOU HOLD ON TO
PAIN YOU WON'T HAVE
SPACE FOR JOY.

YOU CAN'T GRAB AND HOLD AT THE SAME TIME.
Let it go. Your ability to love reveals your capacity
to be loved.

SOMETIMES PAIN IS A SIGN OF VICTORY.

WHAT YOU CAN GIVE AWAY IN YOUR BROKENNESS becomes what you will conquer in your testimony. Your pain is your victory.

I'M NOT PERFECT. I'M LOVED PERFECTLY!

GIVE YOURSELF SPACE AND GRACE. IT'S OK TO struggle, just stay willing to continue. A stoplight doesn't indicate the end of the journey, it's a resting place to clear the streets of our lives. You don't have to be superman, be a man who finds strength in the SUPER.

It's never too late if you're alive.

DID YOU KNOW YOUR BEST DAYS ARE IN FRONT of you? Move forward, go for It!! It's never too late and there's no limit to greatness. There is no arrival, only the destinations we find along the never-ending journey of true success; growth, purpose and a maximized life. Love yourself. Just imagine the possibilities, then live them.

BE CAREFUL WHO YOU HURT, NOT EVERYONE IS REPLACEABLE.

TAKING RESPONSIBILITY FOR YOUR ACTIONS GIVES you the second chance you may not deserve.

Today I hate living.
Today I'm not happy.
Today I feel
unattractive.
Today life is hard.
Today I'm broke.
Today I'm sick.

BUT... Today
is Temporary.

DON'T ALLOW A TEMPORARY SITUATION TO DEFINE your ENTIRE lifetime. You'll overcome. Honestly there is no arrival. A lot of people with reputation, old and new fame/success often are STILL struggling and not doing as well as it appears. In a generation full of selfie highlights it can become confusing and often leads to the dissatisfaction of one's own life, but we must put reality into perspective. On every level there is a struggle and if we desire things beyond what we can gain, the celebration of who we are becoming is more than enough. TODAY YOU'RE ALIVE AND ABLE!

Just because
you're not
ready doesn't
mean you're not
qualified.
Let the areas
that need growth
fuel your journey,
not detour it.

TOO OFTEN WE LET OUR STRUGGLES DICTATE
our success. Get free! Flourish!

DON'T SETTLE FOR TEMPORARY HIGHS WHEN YOU NEED A PERMANENT FIX. NUMBNESS DOESN'T ELIMINATE PROBLEMS, TRANSFORMATION DOES.

THE AREAS YOU FIND YOURSELF WASTING TIME IN are generally the areas of your low self-image.

PRAYER: LORD LET ME SEE MY VALUE TODAY SO I don't prostitute my worth and give myself away to that which can't afford the convictions of my heart.

GOD CAN'T FILL YOU IF YOU ARE FULL OF YOURSELF.

THE PROBLEM ISN'T GOD'S AVAILABILITY IT'S OUR accessibility. The blessing of humility is that it makes room where pride takes up space; stubbornness refuses the need for change and growth. We can't let our puffed up minds overlook the holes we have embraced. Today let's pour our own "wisdom" out and receive the gift of not knowing at all. Let the weak say "I am strong."

DIED BUT
NOT DEAD

THE BLESSING OF TRAGEDY IS THAT WE COME TO FIND WHAT MATTERS.

YOUR HEART IS INDEED BROKEN BUT NOT BEYOND REPAIR.

THE PAIN YOU FEEL FROM A BROKEN HEART IS a reflection on just how much love you hold. As you pour out your pain know love is flowing and healing. You're going to be OKAY.

YOU CAN'T BREAK THROUGH WHAT YOU DON'T RUN INTO. DON'T AVOID OBSTACLES, CRASH INTO THEM! YOU'RE BIGGER.

ALIGNMENT PRODUCES THE VELOCITY to breakthrough.

Your willingness is greater than your tendency to fail.

THE DESIRE TO BE BETTER IS THE SEED TO HEALING. Making a WILLING effort to plant it in the soil of change is all it takes to rebuild the forest of your life. Past, current or future trials cannot overtake a willing heart. The truth "God judges the heart not the actions" isn't an escape from self-accountability, it's the freedom within it.

Being where God has called you is more impactful than being where the world can see you. Embrace YOUR purpose.

WHEN YOU STOP CHASING THE DREAMS of others you can wake up and live for your purpose.

WHAT GIVES
YOU PURPOSE
MAY NOT MAKE
YOU POPULAR.

AN EGO IS A TERRIBLE THING TO WASTE.

143

Don't make rejection your failure.

IT'S DIFFICULT DISCOVERING NEW AND HEALTHIER ways of thinking but it's quintessential to your vitality. Let everything you go through build a better you. Acknowledge yesterday but don't dwell in it. If faced with an obstacle today, have hope for tomorrow. Through it all, remember your life is designed to overcome. To truly overcome you have to be tested with things to overcome. It's hard but you're stronger.

TESTIMONY

5 YEARS AGO TODAY I DIED.

FACED DEATH IN 2010, POSTED 2015

JOHN 10:10 ".... I HAVE COME THAT THEY MAY HAVE LIFE, and that they may have it more abundantly." God and my faith in Him have been my rock. After a rare twisting of my small intestine, caused by nothing specific, I suffered through 4 major surgeries, 7 blood transfusions, and heart failure. I weighed 105lbs, was on tons of medication, in a coma for 4 days, and had 16ft of my 20ft of intestines removed. I was supposed to never eat again by mouth and I had a 10% chance of living (recovery didn't even stand a chance). I almost slipped away twice during surgery. Here I am today, 5 years later by the grace, love and power of God and His spirit. I'm alive because He is alive!

I WAS ALREADY A MAN OF FAITH WHO proclaimed God's word and this happened to me but not without grace and purpose. This was an opportunity to display my faith for all. All saw God keep me alive and now all of you have seen Him lead me to thrive. I don't have it all but I have my life and I will never take it or my purpose for granted. I'm here to do work and when I'm gone that work will continue to work for it is THE WORK OF THE LORD. Thank you Alllll who stood by me during that time and through the years, you were arms when my surrender was weary. Happy 5th birthday to me.

147

TESTIMONY IS GREATER THAN SUCCESS BECAUSE IT DOESN'T JUST SHOW PEOPLE THE PLATFORM, IT REVEALS TO THEM HOW TO GET THERE. BE PROUD OF YOUR JOURNEY.

PART IV.

JOURNEY WITH PURPOSE

PURPOSE, POWER AND ACTIVATION!

HERE BUT FOR A MOMENT BUT THE LEGACY IS ETERNAL.

I AM MIGHTY!

WHEN YOU KNOW WHO YOU ARE YOU CAN EXIST to impact the world not just live in it. Who you are isn't always found in "what you do" or who you think you are to be and it's rarely found in who others say you are. Who you are is found in the cocoon of pure Love, divine creation and the understanding of your purpose.

A LIGHT DOESN'T TURN OFF BECAUSE IT'S DARK.

IT ILLUMINATES!

DON'T BECOME A PRODUCT OF YOUR circumstances, obstacles or environment. CHANGE THEM! Lights best shine in darkness. Use every opportunity to light up your life and you will find a peace within that burns a trail.

If we'd stop waiting for tragedy to hit to pray, Maybe our prayers could prevent some of it altogether. It's a war, Not a fad.

HASHTAGS DON'T CHANGE THE WORLD AS MUCH AS people do. Let's make an INTENTIONAL effort to love. Let's live PROACTIVELY to accomplish good on earth. We don't have to be victims when our faith and love can wage war! Be not afraid, you were born a winner. Make a vow to do your part and change the world around you for better. Will you make the CHOICE to reach?

WHILE I'M HERE I'M
GOING TO SERVE
/ WIN / LEARN
/ FIGHT WITH FAITH
/ BELIEVE
/ BE HEALTHY
/ BE ACCOUNTABLE
/ DO WHAT I CAN.

MAKE EVERY MOMENT AND PORTION OF YOUR LIFE
count, for it's not the platform that reveals who
you are but how you LIVED to get there. You
deserve to live as your GREATest SELF. Share that
person with the world, share that person with
yourself.

YOU HAVE TO FIRST LEAVE THE LIFE YOU'RE LIVING, TO LIVE THE LIFE YOU WANT. DON'T DIE IN YOUR GREATNESS, LIVE IT!

WAITING TO GO WHILE YOU'RE ALREADY EQUIPPED is like locking a high-quality car in a garage. A car was never created to SIT, but to drive. It's not until we place the car on the road that the beauty of its design can

FUNCTION; IT'S BATTERY CAN EVEN RECHARGE itself! Even the most expensive and beautiful car is of no use if it won't drive anywhere. DRIVE your life, you'll figure out the roads as you go and learn the way.

NO.

NO. LEARN ITS POWER AND CONFIDENCE. WHAT you make yourself available to by default makes you unavailable to something else. Everything must have purpose, everything must add. Everything must propel growth. All things are Life.

THERE'S NOTHING TO FINISH IF YOU NEVER START.

LIFE GETS BETTER WHEN WE GET BETTER.
We often pray for more and long to breakthrough to reach a higher level, yet don't want
the responsibility of faith and becoming it takes.
We must stop making excuses, start making
plans and FINISHING THEM. You can't blame
YOUR LIFE on anyone. Life happens out of your
control sometimes, but You have the power to
respond to whatever it brings. Gain control.
How will you respond? If you won't find the
courage to be DISCIPLINED and go after goals
until COMPLETION, you aren't qualified to
receive/manage them.

If your light doesn't illuminate people at best you'll be seen when you were created to show others how to see themselves.

IF THE PEOPLE WHO ARE SUPPOSEDLY MENTORING you invest more energy ensuring you see them than they do SERVING YOU and nurturing the leader in you, you need new relationships. Identity is your stamp. You don't need approval to exist and trials don't disqualify your conquest. A Leader should empower others to surpass their success.

159

WHEN YOU ARE CALLED, ANSWERING RELEASES YOUR VOICE.

DON'T DWELL ON WHAT YOU'RE GOING THROUGH, focus on who YOU ARE BECOMING.

As difficult as it is to embrace your call, do it. You may cry but each tear is supplying the ocean your life will sail upon!

YOU CAN ONLY GIVE WHAT YOU'RE WILLING TO BECOME.

SOMETIMES WHAT WE WANT HAS TO FIND US AND THAT ONLY HAPPENS WHEN WE FIRST CHANGE INTO THE PERSON IT'S DESIGNED FOR.

IT BEGINS IN YOU.

USE YOUR INFLUENCE TO BIRTH A WEALTH OF LIFE.

WATER THE GROUND
WHERE THERE'S SEED.

OUT OF ALL THE
GRAINS OF SAND,
NOT ONE IS THE SUN.

TOO MANY LEADERS TRYNNA BE STARS WHEN THEY ARE SUPPOSED TO BE LIGHTS.

LIGHT ILLUMINATES, IT DOESN'T JUST SHINE.

THOSE WHO OVERLOOK YOU ARE MEANT TO. DON'T FOCUS ON THEM SO MUCH THAT YOU ALSO BEGIN TO OVERLOOK YOURSELF. FOCUS ON THE BIGGER PICTURE/PURPOSE.

PARADISE
IS FOUND
ON THE
ISLAND
OF YOUR
FAITH.

#CarryTheLove.

WE MUST USE OUR GIFTS AND LIVES TO BECOME vehicles of love not just vessels of temporary entertainment. How can YOU use your life to #CarryTheLove?

THE ONLY FAILURE IS NOT BELIEVING.

WHY PLACE A LIMIT ON WHAT YOU HAVEN'T EVEN lived yet? Don't fear the future, shape yourself in it. Success isn't receiving all that we want but remaining willing to become who we need to be to maintain it. This is why the opportunity to believe is true success, because we can't gain what we never believed existed and we can't lose what we already know we have. If we lose ourselves to hope, we can find ourselves in impossibilities because we discover new levels of strength, and that's success and worth.

A STAGE
WITHOUT LIGHTS
BUT ILLUMINATING
A THOUSAND
FACES.

YOU CAN ENJOY LIFE FROM ANY PLATFORM because in purpose what elevates you aren't the opportunities you gain but the opportunities you take to be you exactly WHERE GOD has called you to be.

JOURNEY
& OBSTACLES

WIN.

THE RACE REVEALS THE WINNER IN YOU!
Embrace what you face.

Don't mistake the vehicle for the destination.

WE TOO OFTEN TAKE PRIDE IN WHAT WE'RE DOING and it can stifle who we need to become and/or where we are going. Live full, live a little higher. If we drink the glory, the vehicles given as a resource replace the source and we will eventually run out of gas before we ever reach the place of prosperity.

A BRIDGE OR A HALLWAY?

BRIDGE THE TESTIMONIES OF YOUR LIFE AND you'll always find the road to victory. Where there is a story, there is hope. Never allow your past to hinder you, let it build bridges and move you forward.

HOW YOU SEE THE WORLD DETERMINES THE WORLD YOU'LL LIVE IN.

WHAT WE LOOK AT BECOMES BIGGER.
Our perspective can either reveal the way
or stop at what's blocking it.

A treasure in
a faraway land.
Find the lock
in London.

THE GREATEST TREASURES ARE OFTEN FOUND IN hidden places. Those who find the patience to seek and endure are those worthy to be found.

PREPARE
FOR GLORY.

THE JOURNEY IS THE DESTINATION AND EACH STEP
unlocks the hero inside. Be MIGHTY.

IF YOU STAY COMMITTED TO YOUR DREAM, YOUR DREAM WILL STAY COMMITTED TO YOU, BECAUSE...

YOU ARE THE DREAM!

WE TOO OFTEN GIVE UP WHERE WE SHOULD STAND up. There is no failure. Win or lose, we exist. The things that don't work out still work for us when we let every part of our lives fuel our growth. When the goal is the reward we're limited to what we can gain, when WE are the reward we're free to push the limits. Don't give up because it's hard, become stronger. Stand on the hard obstacles and overcome them to DEVELOP, not just receive.

My message is greater than my platform. My life is created with purpose. There is no need to compare what was never meant to be the same, so I celebrate my route and everything I can BECOME, not simply receive.

WE ALL HAVE MOMENTS WHERE WE FEEL WE should be more visible, but I've learned that we don't need to see the wind to feel its beauty. The summation of a clear liquid can still form waves. Even when I can't see God working, He is near and moving my life forward. If you're feeling underrated or under-celebrated know you are loved and moving places AS YOU embrace that reality. Love does not fail, love yourself and win!

GET TIRED.

WHEN YOU REALLY GET TIRED YOU STOP PUTTING up with excuses and start living for solutions. Sometimes you have to reach the end of the road to get off the path of convenience and walk the road of growth. One may be easier but leads to nowhere, the other is a journey but there's no limit to the places you can go. The problem may not be you but the vehicle you tried to arrive in, discover you're the healthiest vehicle and not only will you gain new value but realize there's only room for ONE: purpose, fuel, time.

BE MORE EXCITED TO GROW THAN GO.

WHEN YOU MAKE THE "DESTINATION" THE ONLY place of excitement, you remain incomplete and in a constant need to ARRIVE to be successful. When the journey is your peace, even once you arrive, you will have grown enough to expand. Arrive again. I've learned there is no arrival, for where I'm maximized in faith and hard work I am right where I need to be. There are MANY destinations of GROWTH.

Don't Mistake the Rivers of your life for a lake, you're flowing somewhere!

RIVERS JOURNEY AND FLOW TO OCEANS WHERE lakes merely sit in one location. Know you're flowing somewhere. It's hard but it's possible and adding up to something. Don't give up! Let the tears you cry and the sweat you pour fill the oceans your life will sail upon. Read: Ecclesiastes 1:7.

Obstacles
are your
Opportunity
to see God.

THE HIGHER THE MOUNTAIN, THE BETTER THE VIEW.

YOUR OBSTACLE IS NOT YOUR DEFEAT.

THE NEED FOR GROWTH DOESN'T DETOUR YOUR success, it just ensures it will be lasting. Let the journey build you, not kill you. Live a little higher than the mountains and you will soar through life.

WARNING SIGNS AREN'T THERE TO CAUSE DEFEAT BUT TO GUIDE YOU SAFELY ALONG THE ROCKY PATHS. YOUR OBSTACLE ISN'T YOUR DESTINATION.

WITH THE RIGHT PERSPECTIVE, LIFE BECOMES a little bit more beautiful.

We spend more energy being mad at our obstacles than seeking the peace to overcome them. When we make what matters bigger, we flourish.

When your faith lacks,
your ability to create
is hindered and
fear of the unknown
settles in, becoming
your only reality.
Having hope moves
your faith to become
a tool and allows what
didn't exist to be
BUILT – limitless
possibility.

WHAT ARE YOU WAITING FOR? DON'T ALLOW THE LENGTH OF THE DRIVE TO DETOUR YOU FROM MAKING THE JOURNEY. FIND FAITH TO TRAVEL AND ARRIVE TO THE OTHER SIDE OF YOUR FEARS.

THE TOP WITHOUT
THE BOTTOM HOLDS
NO VALUE BECAUSE
THE STEPS IT TAKES
TO GET THERE ARE
WHAT DETERMINE
THE HEIGHT OF WHAT
YOU'RE STANDING ON.

IN facing our problems we become more like God, because we don't just receive the answer, we learn to figure out the solution.

YOU CAN DO IT!

I'VE LEARNED THE KEY TO BREAKING THROUGH is becoming strong enough to overcome my obstacles. When you know your purpose, each situation only makes you stronger so you can be a testimony not a failed test. Tests are given to reveal what we've learned. Look within to win!

CONQUER, DON'T COWARD! GROWTH EXISTS IN THE SPACE OF OVERCOMING OUR PROBLEMS, NOT SIMPLY IN THEM JUST DISAPPEARING.
GO THROUGH.

ARE YOU PRAYING THAT ALL OF YOUR PROBLEMS and obstacles vanish or for YOU TO GROW BIG enough to overcome them? If you're simply praying for your trials to disappear you haven't matured to the place of promotion. Often, as WE GET LARGER our problems get smaller and we gain the ABILITY TO CRUSH that which is beneath us. This is why the tests of life shape us, for when we pass not only do our problems get solved but we also come out wiser, BETTER and stronger. Adjust your prayer, look within to win!

✩ ✩ ✩

GOD'S POWER IS MADE PERFECT IN IMPERFECT CIRCUMSTANCES.

OBSTACLES ALLOW DISCOVERY. IF LIFE NEVER presented what is beneath us we wouldn't come to know how high we can stand. God is complete and lacking nothing, so when we lack and run by faith into His presence we discover our wholeness through his loving strength. Faith is not our enemy, the fear to hope is.

THE WAY
OF ROYALTY

HUMILITY gives To live, PRIDE Takes To win.

DESIRE THE SUMMATION OF YOUR LIFE TO NOT BE a resume of what you did, but a testimony of how and who you loved. Being self-consumed doesn't create space to love another because you've withheld it all to love yourself. In a shiny world, I'd rather be a light. Humility is the aim, love is true gain.

Jesus humbly came and led who followed. He never fought for approval, he lived in confidence. He never took account of his doings, He stayed accountable to Love. He's the most famous there ever was.

YOUR PLATFORM IS A TOOL, SIMPLY THAT. DON'T get lost in the hype of your success, it's all vanity. In time there will be new, epic people and greater inventions. If you're so focused on being seen you'll miss the opportunity to give the light of love that will always be REMEMBERED.

HUMILITY IS THE TRUE SIGN OF SUCCESS.

IF YOU LACK HUMILITY, YOU LACK LOVE. IF YOU lack love, what you're building has no purpose. Purpose that doesn't exist beyond SELF isn't purpose at all, it's pride - and I don't mean confidence. Real kings and queens build kingdoms, not simply castles.

FIND THE PURITY TO WANT
FOR PEOPLE MORE THAN
YOU WANT THEM. DON'T
MAKE IT ABOUT WHAT
YOU'RE RECEIVING BUT
WHAT YOU'RE GIVING.

IF WE ALL GAVE, WE WOULD ALL HAVE.
Purify your actions and analyze the integrity
of them. Be good for real.

My desire is to always maintain a PuRE HEART.

"THE PURE IN HEART SHALL SEE GOD," MATTHEW 5:7 #Bible The more time we spend with God the easier it is to see Him. As we look at Him, we can understand the image we were created in. Such identity propels life to be empowered, have meaning and above all, be lived from Love.

True success is inner wisdom and challenge, not the platforms of others' praises.
Push YOUrself.

LOVE YOURSELF ENOUGH TO GROW. DON'T LIMIT your purpose to praise. What we allow to validate us is what we'll need to keep on living. If what we need to live doesn't move us forward we will become the walking dead.

IN HOPING FOR WHAT
YOU DESIRE DON'T LACK
GRATITUDE FOR WHAT
YOU ALREADY HAVE.
DON'T WAIT FOR THE
DREAM TO MANIFEST
TO BE EXCELLENT.

RIGHT WHERE YOU ARE, WITH WHATEVER JOB, be excellent. The process is more about you than the opportunity.

Accountability in responsibility.

THE BEST TEACHERS ARE THOSE WHO DO NOT DO IT for validation or accreditation. To selflessly give for the advancement of another is leadership. As a teacher, the classroom isn't an opportunity to shine as much as it is the responsibility to give light.

SEX IS A POOR SUBSTITUTE FOR LOVE.

DISCOVER WHAT YOU TRULY NEED AND DON'T prostitute your heart for a counterfeit return.

YOU CAN'T WIN IF YOU DON'T FIRST EMBRACE THE FIGHT.

IN WILLINGNESS YOU HAVE THE OPPORTUNITY TO become the answer to the problems you see. What you can see reveals who you need to be. Where you battle most is where you are destined to testify in victory. If you can make it through, many will know they can too.

BOSS VS. LEADER

LEADING ISN'T ABOUT BEING IN CHARGE BUT leading people to find the leader in them. To lead effectively you must take the focus off of you.

LIGHTS CAN BE BLINDING IF YOU LOOK INTO THEM. DON'T GET CAUGHT UP IN YOUR OWN HYPE AND LIGHT, GIVE THEM AWAY. DON'T JUST SHINE, ILLUMINATE!

DON'T SACRIFICE THE INGREDIENTS TO GAIN A FINISHED PRODUCT. LIFE IS NOT FOUND IN WHAT IT LOOKS LIKE, BUT WHAT IT'S MADE OF.

SETTLING FOR THE FACE VALUE OF ANYTHING lacks the substance required to produce it. Don't envy another person's life, for you don't know what it cost to receive it. It may require a debt you would never want to own. Don't take the short cut of a processed life, live organically pure and whole.

UNLOCK THE MIGHT IN YOU

VISION RECOGNIZES A DESTINATION AND CREATES a path to get there, otherwise you'll settle for the postcards of your dreams. It's worth it all to live it all - your best life. While many understand life could be better they stop at the comfort zone of inspiration or void fillers. I agree they sometimes get the job done but it's never lasting nor brings a sense of wholeness. For that reason we can't stop at inspiration, we must seek those things that cause transformation. Desire sustained is a difficult process in life's constant growing but remaining willing to embrace trials, challenge ourselves, love ourselves and love others will carry us to live according to the might in us instead of the fight around us. That vision will be sharpened with each swing of the sword for we are mighty, you are mighty and the need for growth never disqualifies where we already are. We've come far. Remember, the beauty of transformation is often at first glance scary because that which is truly beautiful is new; what hasn't been seen. Don't fear the challenges in you and don't run from the changes that need to take place around you, you're just becoming more BEAUTIFUL!

FOR MORE MYKELL:

#MightyMykell
#Carrythelove
#TheWayofRoyalty

THIS SPACE IS TO WRITE WHATEVER POSITIVITY YOU ARE DECLARING FOR YOUR LIFE.

MIGHTY DECLARATIONS | #MightyDeclarations

ABOUT THE AUTHOR

BORN IN RIVERSIDE, CALIFORNIA, MYKELL WILSON has always allowed purpose to steer his passions. Beginning his journey at California State University, Los Angeles, on a path to become a senator, he felt a call to work in the entertainment industry. After college, he gained the courage to switch his focus, at first directing his energy towards acting before taking a risk with dance. After much sacrifice and hard work, Mykell's career has taken him on world tours, allowed him to assist choreographers and choreograph for the likes of Britney Spears, and other international superstars. Mykell has been seen on television dancing for the legendary Prince, Justin Bieber and Neil Patrick Harris, among many other artists.

THOUGH SUCCESSFUL, HIS MISSION HAS NEVER BEEN about fame, but about purpose. He invests much of his time in ministry, leading worship, public speaking, aiding the community, and using his platform to reach the hearts of people. The desire to be a light in a dark world motivates Mykell to remain self-aware and evaluate himself on a regular basis. Just like any other person, he has to live the human experience and he has found the best way to do so is with hope and faith.

THIS BOOK IS AN ACCUMULATION OF VARIOUS writings from his social platforms, often inspired from his own experiences. A public figure, an artist, he is known by many as Mighty Mykell and wants you, too, to find the source of might within yourselves.